The Unschooling Unmanual

Nanda Van Gestel

Jan Hunt

Daniel Quinn

Rue Kream

Earl Stevens

Kim Houssenloge

John Holt

Mary Van Doren

Edited by Jan and Jason Hunt

Book design by Jason Hunt

The Natural Child Project

naturalchild.org

Library and Archives Canada Cataloguing in Publication

The unschooling unmanual / Nanda van Gestel ... [et al.] ; edited by Jan
and Jason Hunt ; book design by Jason Hunt.

Includes bibliographical references.
ISBN 978-0-9685754-5-1 (bound)

1. Home schooling. 2. Non-formal education. 3. Education — Parent participation.
I. Van Gestel, Nanda, 1964- II. Hunt, Jan, 1942- III. Hunt, Jason, 1981-.

LC40.U58 2008   371.04'2   C2007-907656-4

Front and back cover design and book layout by Jason Hunt. Cover photo of Jason,
age 4, by Jan Hunt. Back cover photo of Koen and Jochem by Nanda Van Gestel.

"Schooling: The Hidden Agenda" was presented at the Houston Unschoolers Group
Family Learning Conference, October 2000. © 2000 Daniel Quinn.

Jan Hunt's articles "The Natural Love of Learning" and "How Do We Know They're
Learning?" are adapted from *The Natural Child: Parenting From the Heart*. © 2001.

Rue Kream's articles "Why Choose Unschooling?" and "What About College?"
are reprinted from her book *Parenting a Free Child: An Unschooled Life*. © 2005.

"Every Waking Hour" is excerpted from *Learning All the Time* by John Holt. © 2005.
Reprinted by arrangement with Basic Books, a member of the Perseus Books
Group (perseusbooks.com). All rights reserved.

"Mary's Memoirs" by Mary Van Doren originally appeared in *Growing Without
Schooling* in the 1980s. Reprinted with permission of Holt Associates/*Growing
Without Schooling* (holtgws.com).

To order *The Unschooling Unmanual* directly from the publishers, and for more
information about this book, visit naturalchild.org/unmanual.

Dedicated to John Caldwell Holt
1923-1985

"Little children love the world. That is why they are so good at learning about it. For it is love, not tricks and techniques of thought, that lies at the heart of all true learning. Can we bring ourselves to let children learn and grow through that love?"

John Holt

Contents

Why Choose Unschooling?

by Rue Kream

"A person's freedom of learning is part of his freedom of thought, even more basic than his freedom of speech."

– John Holt

Why did you choose unschooling rather than some other form of homeschooling?

I always knew that the way "everybody" lived didn't feel right to me. I used to imagine that, when I grew up, I would live on an island with my family. From a very young age I struggled to understand what life really meant. As I grew, I came up with some answers. Life for me is truly feeling the earth underneath me and seeing the things around me. It is enjoying every moment with the people I love. It is making another person smile. It is thinking and dreaming, feeling pain and feeling joy.

When Dagny was a baby, I started to ask myself new questions. Does it matter if we know our multiplication tables? Is accumulation of knowledge the goal of life? Should there *be* a goal of life? Why should we spend her childhood apart from each other when we both want so much to be together? Can we step off the well-worn path and find our own way?

When I learned that unschooling was a possibility, I was thrilled that we could continue to live as we had been since Dagny was born. I found the answers to my questions, which in reality I had known all along. Children belong with their families. Nothing is more important than living in connection with the ones you love and sharing life's experiences. We can't help but learn as we live full and interesting lives together.

When we rejected the kind of life that comes with a road map, we were able to question what it was we wanted from our lives, and to determine what we do not want. We want joy. We want to know that we lived consciously and in the moment. We do not want to mold our children. We want them to have the freedom to choose their lives. We do not want to ever feel that we wasted time we could have spent together.

Children belong with their families.

Our major reasons for unschooling have nothing to do with academics, but of course there are reasons we choose not to teach our children. We believe that children (humans) seek out knowledge in the same way they seek out fun or food, and we believe that adults can do a lot to interfere with that desire to learn. We don't believe that repetition is necessary or that there is a list of things that every person needs to know. We believe that turning the relationship of parent and child into a relationship between teacher and student is detrimental. We want our children to own their learning and to learn for their own reasons, not to please a teacher.

Jon and I have determined what it is we live by, what matters, and what does not. It has evolved and will continue to evolve as we face new challenges and joys in our lives. We want to choose the lives we lead, and we want our children to have the opportunity to do the same.

Ultimately I'd say that the reason we choose to unschool is because we want our children to be truly free.

"School always appeared to me like a prison, and I could never make up my mind to stay there, when the sunshine was inviting, the sea smooth, and when it was such a joy to run about in the free air, or to paddle around in the water."

Claude Monet

The Natural Love of Learning

by Jan Hunt

The main element in successful unschooling is trust. We trust our children to know when they are ready to learn and what they are interested in learning. We trust them to know how to go about learning. Parents commonly take this view of learning during the child's first two years, when he is learning to stand, walk, talk, and to perform many other important and difficult things, with little help from anyone. No one worries that a baby will be too lazy, uncooperative, or unmotivated to learn these things; it is simply assumed that every baby is born wanting to learn the things he needs to know in order to understand and to participate in the world around him. These one- and two-year-old experts teach us several principles of learning:

Children are naturally curious and have a built-in desire to learn first-hand about the world around them.

John Holt, in his book *How Children Learn*, describes the natural learning style of young children:

"The child is curious. He wants to make sense out of things, find out how things work, gain competence and control over himself and his environment, and do what he can see other people doing. He is open, perceptive, and experimental. He does not merely observe the world around him. He does not shut himself off from the strange, complicated world around him, but tastes it, touches it, hefts it, bends it, breaks it. To find out how reality works, he works on it. He is bold. He is not afraid of making mistakes. And he is patient. He can tolerate an extraordinary amount of uncertainty, confusion, ignorance, and suspense. ... School is not a place that gives much time, or opportunity, or reward, for this kind of thinking and learning."

Children know best how to go about learning something.

If left alone, children will know instinctively what method is best for them. Caring and observant parents soon learn that it is safe and appropriate to trust this knowledge. Such parents say to their baby, "Oh, that's interesting! You're learning how to crawl downstairs by facing backwards!" They do not say, "That's the wrong way." Perceptive parents are aware that there are many different ways to learn something, and they trust their children to know which ways are best for them.

Children need plentiful amounts of quiet time to think.

As John Holt noted in *Teach Your Own*, "Children who are good at fantasizing are better both at learning about the world and at learning to cope with its surprises and disappointment. It isn't hard to see why this should be so. In fantasy we have a way of trying out situations, to get some feel of what they might be like, or how we might feel in them, without having to risk too much. It also gives us a way of coping with bad experiences, by letting us play and replay them in our mind until they have lost much of their power to hurt, or until we can make them come out in ways that leave us feeling less defeated and foolish."

But fantasy requires time, and time is the most endangered commodity in our lives. Fully-scheduled school hours and extracurricular activities leave little time for children to dream, to think, to invent solutions to problems, to cope with stressful experiences, or simply to fulfill the universal need for solitude and privacy.

Children are not afraid to admit ignorance and to make mistakes.

When Holt invited toddlers to play his cello, they would eagerly attempt to do so; schoolchildren and adults would invariably decline. Unschooling children, free from the intimidation of public embarrassment and failing marks, retain their openness to new exploration. Children learn by asking questions, not by answering them. Toddlers ask many questions, and so do school children — until about grade three. By that time, many of them have learned an unfortunate fact: that in school, it can be more important for self-protection to hide one's ignorance about a subject than to learn more about it, regardless of one's curiosity.

Children learn by asking questions,
not by answering them.

Children take joy in the intrinsic values of whatever they are learning.

There is no need to motivate children through the use of extrinsic rewards, such as high grades or stars, which suggest to the child that the activity itself must be difficult or unpleasant; otherwise, why is a reward, which has nothing to do with the matter at hand, being offered? The wise parent says, "I think you'll enjoy this book", not "If you read this book, you'll get a cookie."

Children learn best about getting along with other people through interaction with those of all ages.

No parents would tell their baby, "You may only spend time with those children whose birthdays fall within six months of your own. Here's another two-year-old to play with."

In his book *Dumbing Us Down*, New York State Teacher of the Year John Taylor Gatto states, "It is absurd and anti-life to be part of a system that compels you to sit in confinement with people of exactly the same age and social class. That system effectively cuts you off from the immense diversity of life and the synergy of variety; indeed, it cuts you off from your own past and future, sealing you in a continuous present ... ."

Children learn best about the world through first-hand experience.

No parent would tell her toddler, "Let's put that caterpillar down and get back to your book about caterpillars." Unschoolers learn directly about the world. Our son describes unschooling as "learning by doing instead of being taught". Ironically, the most common objection about unschooling is that children are "being deprived of the real world".

Children need and deserve ample time with their family.

Gatto cautions us, "Between schooling and television, all the time children have is eaten up. That's what has destroyed the American family." Many unschooling parents feel that family cohesiveness is perhaps the most meaningful benefit of the experience. Just as I saw his first step and heard his first word, I have the honor and privilege of sharing my son's world and thoughts. Over the years, I have discovered more from him about life, learning, and love, than from any other source. The topic we seem to be learning the most about is the nature of learning itself. I sometimes wonder who learns more in unschooling families, the parents or the children!

Stress interferes with learning.

As Albert Einstein wrote in his *Autobiographical Notes*, "It is a very grave mistake to think that the enjoyment of seeing and searching can be promoted by means of coercion." When a one-year-old falls down while learning to walk, we say, "Good try! You'll catch on soon!" No caring parent would say, "Every baby your age should be walking. You'd better be walking by Friday!"

Most parents understand how difficult it is for their children to learn something when they are rushed, threatened, or given failing grades. John Holt warned that "we think badly, and even perceive badly, or not at all, when we are anxious or afraid … when we make children afraid, we stop learning dead in its tracks."

While infants and toddlers teach us many principles of learning, schools have adopted quite different principles, due to the difficulties inherent in teaching a large number of same-age children in a compulsory setting. The structure of school — required attendance, school-selected topics and books, and constant checking of the child's progress — assumes that children are not natural learners, but must be compelled to learn through the efforts of others.

Natural learners do not need such a structure. The success of self-directed learning (unschoolers regularly outperform their schooled peers on measures of achievement, socialization, confidence, and self-esteem) strongly suggests that structured approaches inhibit both learning and personal development. Because unschooling follows principles of natural learning, children retain the curiosity, enthusiasm, and love of learning that every child has at birth.

Unschooling, as Holt writes in *How Children Learn,* is a matter of faith. "This faith is that by nature people are learning animals. Birds fly; fish swim; humans think and learn. Therefore, we do not need to motivate children into learning by wheedling, bribing, or bullying. We do not need to keep picking away at their minds to make sure they are learning. What we need to do — and all we need to do — is to give children as much help and guidance as they need and ask for, listen respectfully when they feel like talking, and then get out of the way. We can trust them to do the rest."

A Way of Life

The whole idea of natural learning has evolved over the past few years from something we thought would be good for our children, to a way of life; part of a way of life, actually, which is itself still evolving for us.

I think freedom is the key to all of this — freedom to raise our children the best way we can, freedom for us and our children to learn and grow at the right time. With the children, I find more and more that we must let them do what they feel they need to do. We never know what will come from a particular activity.

One example pointed this out to me very clearly recently. Helen (3) suddenly started making doll beds everywhere, especially in the linen closet. As irritating as I occasionally found this, I didn't say anything about it and somehow was able to leave the sheets and pillowcases as they were, layered with dolls. Now, suddenly, Helen makes the other beds in the house. I feel that she had done some training for it on her own with the dolls, and we were all lucky that I didn't interfere. She doesn't do it every day, but then neither do I.

An Unschooling Adventure
by Nanda Van Gestel

"There is no difference between living and learning ... it is impossible, and misleading, and harmful to think of them as being separate."

John Holt

Our Family

My name is Nanda. I am married to Hans, and together we have four boys: Rutger, Stijn, Jochem, and Koen. We are a Dutch family who left the Netherlands and moved to the U.S., and later Ireland, to be able to unschool our children. We are currently back in the Netherlands.

Our oldest son, Rutger, was born prematurely, and we nearly lost him. There were medical complications, and it was three months before we could bring him home.

Rutger has been called a "special needs" child. We don't like to label anyone — all of our boys are special. My heart told me that if we wanted to make Rutger happy, we needed to focus on his strengths and love him unconditionally. We found that not only is he loving and sensitive, he is also intelligent. We helped him to follow his own interests, and he enriched and deepened our lives in ways we never thought possible. Most of all, he was a happy child.

When Rutger entered school at age five, all of this changed. In just a few months, our bright, confident son had turned into a scared and unhappy child. In school, he couldn't pursue his own interests, and because he wasn't challenged by what was going on in the class-room, he would escape into his own inner world. The teachers responded to this by putting more and more pressure on him — and on me. I spent many hours talking with them, but it didn't help. It became clear to me that they expected children to submit to the school system and sacrifice their own interests, even if that would break their spirit.

I wished with all my heart that we could take care of Rutger's education ourselves. Seeing my child suffer gave me the courage to follow my heart and keep him home; unfortunately, school attendance was mandatory in the Netherlands. We had no idea what would happen next, when the solution came as if by magic — my husband was offered a job in the U.S. On the Internet we learned that homeschooling is legal in all 50 states.

We didn't need long to make up our minds; we sold everything and moved. It was such an eye-opener to us that what is illegal in one country is fully accepted and considered a human right in another. In the Netherlands, people thought of us as irresponsible for wanting to take Rutger out of school; in the U.S. we were admired for taking responsibility for his education. The change we saw in him after our move was almost unbelievable, as if a heavy burden had been lifted off his shoulders. He finally had the freedom to be himself.

Unschooling is more than an education — it's life.

From curriculum-based homeschooling we grew toward unschooling, in which we trust that our children know what they need to learn and when they need to learn it. As George Bernard Shaw wrote, "What we want to see is the child in pursuit of knowledge, not knowledge in pursuit of the child."

It's wonderful to see our children's unique gifts and abilities, and to watch them grow and learn together. Hans and I have learned more in the last several years than ever before, due to all the different topics our children bring up, and all the questions they ask.

Unschooling is more than an education — it's life. In natural learning, everything is connected. Our children have gone from classical music to art, architecture, and ancient Rome, and from there to philosophy, Plato, Pythagoras and mathematics. In this way things make sense, and there is no end to what they can learn; one interest leads into another. Just as babies and toddlers constantly explore the world around them, never growing tired of it, so will unschooling children continue to satisfy their natural curiosity and thirst for knowledge.

As for Rutger, he is doing great — he loves to read and explore, and keeps amazing us with all the things he has learned. He is happy again, and feels proud and confident. Unschooling has liberated us all in many wonderful ways.

Knowledge and Wisdom

While unschooling is natural for children, parents may need to rediscover how easy and joyful learning can be. This didn't come naturally to me at first. Because I went to school myself, part of me still thought that you could only learn if you sat behind a desk and listened to a teacher. Then, when you've gained the teacher's approval in the form of a good grade, you've learned something. But if that were true, how can it be that I don't remember the things I learned this way? And how can it be that the experiences that have really taught me and helped me to grow as a person took place outside of school, in real life?

My father has always said there is a big difference between knowledge and wisdom, and I think he's right. Wisdom is something that we find through life experience; it can't be taught in a classroom. As unschoolers, we live our life and learn from every situation we encounter.

Every day our children learn more about what they can do, what they believe in, and what makes them happy. That's wisdom. Knowledge comes to them because they are curious about the world they live in, because they love to read and to explore, and because they encounter everyone and everything with an open mind and heart.

Freedom

When we do something by choice, we can be creative about it and give it our very best effort. If we choose to do something, we can enjoy it. Feeling coerced to do something is a sure way to take the fun out of it!

The school system is based on making children do things, molding and conditioning them to behave in certain ways. Children "have to" go to school, they "have to" stay in the classroom and they "have to" listen to the teacher. This approach interferes with learning, because we learn best what we are most interested in at the moment. The desire to learn must come from within; forcing children to listen won't make them learn. The use of tests and grades compels students to memorize, at least temporarily, what the teacher has told them. This way it may seem as though the students are learning; in fact they're only learning how to take tests.

The desire to learn must come from within.

Rutger resists pressure even more than I do, and when he attended school, it literally made him ill. The best part of unschooling is that our children are free to learn what they want to, when they want to, and how they want to. We don't have a system; there is no mold that our children have to fit. Instead, unschooling is a celebration of each child's unique personality and abilities. To Rutger, unschooling meant finally being free to be himself.

Rutger wasn't the only one who felt liberated — we all felt free to make our own choices. When Rutger went to school, we all had to fit into the same schedule. I had to get up at a certain time, get my son ready and take him to school. We could no longer go on outings or vacations when we felt like it, and we couldn't accompany my husband on business trips. It was very clear that we all had to adapt to the system. Having Rutger in school drained our energy and put a lot of pressure on our whole family. Now that we're unschooling, we're free to let the day progress naturally, and that makes all of our lives much easier.

Mutual Respect

Some people think that a child's cooperation is something adults are entitled to; they think it is something they can demand. But genuine cooperation cannot be demanded — it can only be earned, and must be given freely. When children feel respected, they want to cooperate.

Children who are raised with trust and respect feel free to express their needs and opinions. When we want our children to do something, or to stop doing something, we don't tell them that they "have to" or "aren't allowed to". Instead, we express our needs and feelings, and listen to theirs, just as we would with an adult friend.

A while ago, Hans visited the home of a colleague who raises his children in the conventional, authoritarian way. My husband was saddened to see how his colleague's children were "seen but not heard". What a difference from a typical day at our house!

When children feel respected,
they want to cooperate.

It can be quite lively and busy at our place, with four boys playing, learning and talking all the time. We really value our children's opinions and ideas, and we love talking with them about different subjects. We find it fascinating to hear what they think and feel. They all have their own opinions, and would find it strange not to be allowed to express them.

The question we should ask ourselves is: What does our society need most — people who will always do as they are asked, or independent, creative thinkers? People who have been dominated from an early age learn to dominate others when they get the chance, while people who are happy about who they are and have self-respect, will respect others.

Attachment Parenting

When I was pregnant and announced that I would quit my job after our baby was born, a lot of people didn't understand. They would ask, "Aren't you afraid you won't be able to talk about anything but booties and diapers?" I think it all depends on our perspective. If we're only aware of the day-to-day routine, and think that parenthood is all about changing diapers and making sure our children are dressed and well-fed, then it could indeed become mind-numbing. When we realize that we're also responsible for our child's emotional well-being, parenting becomes a lot more interesting, and our own capacity for love and compassion grows.

Unschooling allows each child to take their own unique learning path.

When we announced that we wanted to take care of our children's education ourselves, the reactions were often skeptical: "That's a huge responsibility; I would never dare to do it." Or, "How can children learn when they don't go to school?" As with parenting, it all depends on our own personal awareness. We had already experienced what attachment parenting could do for our children and our entire family, and now we wanted to expand that philosophy to their education.

When Rutger could no longer cope with the school system, it gave us a reason to start unschooling. However, the underlying philosophy behind our decision was our holistic approach to parenting and education. Unschooling allows each child to take their own unique learning path. By following their hearts and pursuing their own interests, they learn to take responsibility for their personal growth. Hans and I are there to encourage and assist.

Of course, there are alternative schools that take a holistic approach to education, but they are still schools. Unschooling is like a home-cooked meal, prepared with love, that includes our child's favorite foods, while school is more like a prepackaged meal which may or may not match our child's preferences. No teacher can possibly take each child's unique interests into account, and all schools separate parents from children and siblings from each other. To me, the most important aspect of both parenting and education is the ability to see the loving essence within each child. No one is better at that than a loving parent.

A Healthy Balance

When Rutger attended school, he would come home with one virus infection after another. By the time he was better, the next illness was going around, and we were all sick more often than not. The whole family had trouble staying balanced because we all had to hurry, hurry, hurry just to keep up with the school schedule. And I believe that we are all more prone to illness when we're emotionally out of balance.

Now that we're unschooling, we can set our own schedules. We're free to listen to the subtle signals our bodies are sending us, those "inner voices" that tell us how to stay mentally, emotionally and physically fit. Illnesses like the flu and colds remind us that we need to slow down.

When our whole family was home recovering after a busy period of trying to keep up with everything, it would take time to regain our inner balance. Now that we're unschooling we seldom reach that point, because we can slow down and rest when we need to. In fact we've hardly ever been sick since we started unschooling.

We can slow down and rest when we need to.

It's not so long ago that doctors told us we should feed our babies on a strict schedule, instead of on request. Most mothers now understand that infants know best when they should be fed. Babies know perfectly well when they're hungry, and they always let us know! Why not take it a step further and trust children to know how to go about learning? Children know when they're hungry for information, and they also know when they need processing time.

I used to feel a bit guilty whenever we would spend a rainy day relaxing on the couch, watching movies. After a while I realized that a few of those "nice and easy" days would give us new energy. It's natural for children to listen to the signals of their bodies and to live according to their own rhythms. If we encourage them to trust these feelings, they will be happy and healthy, and will learn in the most natural way.

Natural Reading

I grew up in a family where everyone loved books, and I was often read to. By reading a good book, we can look inside someone's mind and heart. I have always found that the right book will come into my life at the exact right time, but in school I had to read books that someone else had chosen, and it almost destroyed my love for reading.

Because they like to read, our children have learned that there can be many different opinions about a subject. I think that's wonderful, because they don't assume that there is only one way of looking at things — as they might if they were in school. Instead they learn to think for themselves, take all the information they've gathered into account, and form their own opinions.

We visit our local library at least twice a week, and the boys bring long wish lists of books, software and videos they want to check out. Libraries are an unschooler's paradise — we can come and go as we please, there are no tests, and we come home with bags full of books and other materials of our own choosing. In the winter, we sit down to read in front of the fire and drink hot cocoa; in summer, we read in the shade of a big tree with some cool lemonade. The older children often read by themselves, and they also enjoy reading to the younger ones.

The best way to teach children how to read is simply by reading to them.

The best way to teach children how to read is simply by reading to them — as often as we can. When they're ready to read they'll take off on their own. Children can be ready to read at different ages. Rutger was reading by himself at age five; books were his main interest. Stijn didn't read until he was eight, but when he was ready, he learned quickly.

While pressuring a child to read at a certain age may "work", it can create negative associations and jeopardize his future interest in reading. Until a child reads by himself, we can best help him by reading to him without expecting or pushing him to read on his own. In this way we can give our child a lifelong love of reading.

The Arts

I love to draw, but in school art classes we couldn't choose the subject. I remember the time when I had to illustrate a bicycle in great detail. It was so uninteresting to me that it almost made me dislike art. What I liked to draw — and still do — are horses. In art class we didn't draw horses, so I drew them in secret during other lessons. When I look through my old school workbooks, I find many, many sketches of horses, and not much else.

I drew horses in secret.

A while ago one of Stijn's friends invited him to join her after-school art class. Stijn loves drawing and painting, but when I asked if he wanted to go to the class, he decided he would rather keep painting in his own way, so instead we bought new paint and brushes.

While art classes can help us learn new techniques, those are best learned when the child is ready and interested. What is more important is having the freedom to create straight from the heart, without restrictions or judgment. Self-taught people in many fields often produce fresher, more unique, and more creative work than those who have been taught specialized techniques and methods. Nobody has ever told Stijn how you should or shouldn't paint, so he paints from the heart, without being limited by unquestioned rules or traditions.

I remember taking a field trip to an art museum when I was in school. During our visit, we were regularly quizzed, which interfered with our natural exploration and enjoyment. What a difference from the way our children experience a museum visit! While Rutger doesn't draw or paint much, he's a great art lover. He's read many books on famous painters and knows all about their work. He's the one in our family who is most excited when we visit a museum. Whether creating art or appreciating it, we will find the greatest fulfillment when we do it with our heart and soul.

Math in Everyday Life

When we first started unschooling, I soon discovered that children learn best if we let them follow their own interests. I had my doubts about math, though. I couldn't believe that children would find math interesting or fun, because I had never really enjoyed math myself. How wrong I was!

When I tried to teach my children math, they didn't like it either. It didn't matter how much I tried to make it fun. They didn't like it because they couldn't see how math would be of use in their lives. When I stopped trying to teach them, my children showed me that math is everywhere around us. It becomes much more interesting once we stop seeing it as a separate subject, and recognize that it's a part of everyday life.

One night all four boys were gathered around the computer while Jochem was playing a game of Lego Racers. Stijn showed me a paper with lots of numbers written on it. "Look Mom," he said, "we're having a Lego Racers competition. Everyone gets to race three times, and I write down the time of each race. Then I'll add them all up, divide by three, and we'll know who the winner is!"

Math is everywhere around us.

Our boys also love to play board games, especially Monopoly. We play it a lot, and because they enjoy it so much, they're eager to learn the math. For example, players can choose whether to pay a fixed amount of tax or ten per cent of their assets, so the boys wanted to learn all about percentages. This led to an interesting discussion about whether they would rather have a percentage of their dad's salary or the fixed allowance they were getting.

Jochem is the builder in our family. He spends hours creating the most beautiful Lego houses. Koen likes to help his big brother find the Lego bricks he needs in the big bin. "Koen, can you find me a thin white brick with twelve dots?" I heard Jochem ask. "I've got two with six dots for you," Koen answered, "that will work just fine too, won't it?"

Rutger didn't like math in school, but he loves playing the Zoombini computer games. I've played them myself and found them rather difficult. There's pattern finding, problem solving, sorting, graphing and mapping — all to guide the cute little Zoombini characters back to their home. Rutger doesn't find it difficult at all — it's just fun. "Am I really doing math now?" he asked, surprised. "Then I might like math after all."

The Art of Playing

Jochem once said to me, "Mom, did you know that schoolchildren can't play?" When I asked him what he meant, he explained, "Well, whenever we have schoolchildren over, I notice that they run and shout a lot, but they never seem to really play. I think it's because they haven't had much time to themselves, and that's very sad." I was impressed by Jochem's observations, and I've noticed the same pattern myself.

Play is a way of making sense of the world.

Young children have so many commitments and appointments nowadays. How can they find the time and peace of mind to play? No wonder so many of them run around and shout when they have a free moment! I can only agree with Jochem that it's very sad.

Jochem and Koen often play together until they go to bed, and when they wake up the next morning they just continue right where they left off. During the summer, they love to play outside making roads in the sand and driving toy cars over them, or making tiny houses from sticks and leaves. Their little toy characters have all sorts of adventures and "talk" in tiny little voices. In winter, they play the same way inside, with Lego bricks and wooden toys.

One day, I heard screaming upstairs and hurried to see what was wrong. I was sure the boys were fighting. When I entered the room and asked what the matter was, they both looked surprised, and started laughing. "No, Mom," they said, "*we* weren't fighting — these two Lego men are having an argument." I sat down and watched them help the Lego men settle their differences. At that moment I realized that playing is an art. Play is a way of making sense of the world, an opportunity to practice life's many challenges on a smaller scale.

Taking Time

Rutger once said, "I don't understand how children can feel bored, because there are always new books to read." I believe that boredom is a side-effect of the conventional school approach. In school, children are taught *not* to do what they feel like, and *not* to act on a sudden creative impulse or idea. Instead, they are expected to just sit and listen. Then, on weekends and school vacations, they can feel overwhelmed by the large amount of time suddenly available to spend on things they actually like. They might not even remember what most interested them.

Boredom is unknown to a baby or toddler. At that age, children are fascinated with the world around them; they are naturally curious about everything. Unschoolers retain this love of learning, and their natural curiosity will continue to flourish as they grow.

I think it's important to understand that all children may seem bored at times. But if we offer them an activity the minute they show the first sign of boredom, we don't give them the chance to discover what they really want to do. Processing time is just as necessary as active, productive time. If children can be trusted to take the time they need, they will eventually discover what interests them and gives them joy.

It often happens in our family that in moments of inactivity, the most creative and exciting new ideas are born. We have active periods in which we go on trips, work on projects and learn about many new things. We also have quieter periods when we stay mostly at home and think about all we've learned, taking time to process it. Both the active and inactive periods are an essential part of learning.

Friendship

Many people understand that children can learn reading and writing at home, but they worry about socialization. They wonder if unschooling children interact well with others, if they have enough friends, or if they ever feel lonely.

There are many ways in which unschooling children can make friends. Local unschooling support groups offer regular get-togethers and outings. There are opportunities in most communities to meet others sharing similar interests, such as music, dance, sports, and theater. Volunteer work and apprenticeships are often available to match a specific interest. Many families find like-minded friends through attachment parenting and unschooling support groups. And if parents can't find the right group for their family, they can always start their own.

In school, there can be a lot of peer pressure, and because of that, schoolchildren find it important to fit in. Our children don't have this need to conform because they have a strong sense of who they are and what is important to them. They don't feel the need to be accepted by others; they have learned to accept themselves.

It's also important for children to have the chance to spend time alone if they want to. Our boys are very close and love to play and learn together, but they also enjoy playing by themselves. They are excited when other children visit, and they are comfortable alone. There's so much focus on socialization nowadays that we can forget how important it is to have time to oneself. As Thich Nhat Hanh wrote in *A Pebble for Your Pocket*, "Each of you has a hermitage to go to inside — a place to take refuge and breathe. But this does not mean that you are cutting yourself off from the world. It means that you are getting more in touch with yourself."

Unschooling children can be friends with people of all ages.

Unschooling children are free to choose the amount of time they spend with others, as well as the way that time is spent. One of the greatest benefits of unschooling is that children aren't confined to a small group of classmates for friendship, and can be friends with people of all ages.

Joy

These days children go to preschool earlier than ever. I remember people asking us if we had already enrolled Rutger for preschool when he was one year old! "Wouldn't it be great to have some time to yourself?" they would ask.

I'm not surprised that mothers might long for their children to attend school so they can have some peace and quiet. I often see parents busy correcting their child's behavior. That must be pretty tiring! If we can look at our children in a different way, and really enjoy their company, then parenting becomes a pleasure.

One day we had planned to go grocery shopping, but the sun was shining brightly and we decided to go to a park instead. We chose one that has a lake with a nice little sandy beach. We had a picnic lunch, and then we played in the sand, making sandcastles and baking sand "cakes". And when Rutger dropped a ball in the lake, we of course all had to take off our shoes and wade into the water! When we were finished playing, our clothes were a bit wet and we were all covered in sand, but we sure had a wonderful and relaxing afternoon.

Unschooling gives us the opportunity to truly enjoy life with our children.

We still needed groceries, so we stopped at the store on our way home. "Homeschoolers, I suppose?" the lady at the checkout asked. "I can always tell." I was surprised, but when I looked around I could see that we were the only ones with sandy shoes, wet clothes, red cheeks and happy expressions on our faces, on a regular weekday in October.

One of the best advantages of being a parent is that it gives us a great excuse to play! We can build with Lego, make a sandcastle, and have fun at the playground — all in the name of parenthood. If we've forgotten how to play, our children will be happy to remind us. Unschooling gives us the opportunity to truly enjoy life with our children.

Learning from Life

One winter night, our cat died. While that was a sad event, in a way it was also beautiful. She had lived to be 23 — quite a long life for a cat. During the last few months of her life, it became obvious to us all that she wouldn't be with us much longer. Her death didn't come as a surprise, and the ending was very natural. During her last day, we saw her condition quickly worsen. At first I wanted to jump in the car and go to the vet to have it over with as soon as possible.

She wasn't in pain though, and the boys wanted her to be at home, on her pillow in front of the fire, surrounded by all of us. They suggested that we all watch "The AristoCats" to honor her life.

It turned out to be a very special night, with our cat the center of attention. During the movie they all sat with her and said their goodbyes. When the movie was over, our cat took her last breath. She lay on her pillow, surrounded by candles and freshly picked flowers. Every now and then, one of the boys would look at her or touch her, and when we all felt ready, we buried her in the garden. That night, we read a book about the nine lives of a cat.

I remember when I skipped school one morning with a friend of mine because her pony was giving birth. I can still clearly remember how we watched from a corner of the stall while the veterinarian tried to save the pony after the foal was stillborn. I don't remember what lessons we had in school the rest of that day, but I do remember that I had many questions, and that none of them were answered.

Some years ago, one of our horses had a foal, and the boys were present at that magical occasion. At times like that, I'm so happy that our children unschool. We can take all the time we need to experience life fully and learn from these special moments.

Our third son, Jochem, was born while his oldest brother, Rutger, was still attending school. I remember how happy I was that Jochem was born during the Christmas holidays. If he had been born a few weeks earlier or later, Rutger would not have been able to fully enjoy that wondrous time with his newborn brother. Now it's one of his most precious memories.

Dreams

Children learn much more from our actions than from our words. Instead of telling a child to say "please" and "thank you", it's simpler and more respectful to be polite to *them*. True kindness grows within a child only when they are treated with kindness. In the same way, if children see adults reading and learning, their natural curiosity will be nurtured. And by pursuing our dreams, we can inspire our children to follow theirs.

When my husband Hans was a child, he knew he wanted to be a saxophone player. But everyone told him that it wasn't possible to make a living that way, so he gave up on his dream, and chose a business career instead. At age 40, he realized that he feels happiest on stage playing music, and we decided to make his dream a reality.

Unschooling allows children to discover their gifts.

Our U.S. visa was about to expire, so we sold our farm. We had to return to Europe, but we could choose where to settle, and we decided on that as a family. We took a cottage in Ireland so my husband could get out of the "fast lane", and do what he likes best.

Before leaving the U.S., we all made a list of the things that we value most in life, and we found those things in Ireland. We wanted to live surrounded by nature and have animals to care for. Our house in Ireland was bordered by a forest and a stream, and came with a resident pony and cats! It took a lot of courage, but we showed our children that change can be a good thing.

While living in Ireland, we traveled through Europe for several months, and learned many new things. The boys played cavemen after visiting prehistoric sites and became knights after visiting castles. They tasted new foods and heard new languages; made new friends and rekindled old friendships. They learned that they can be happy anywhere in the world, and that they don't have to be afraid of change.

Later, when our boys felt the need to be closer to our extended family and to learn more about their roots, we had an opportunity to move back to the Netherlands (fortunately, regulations have eased somewhat, and families can now request an exemption from school based on holistic parenting beliefs).

I think we all know deep inside what makes us who we are — what our "mission" in life is. We all carry beautiful gifts to share with the world. Unschooling allows children to discover their gifts, and learn whatever they need to learn to have a fulfilling life.

Trust

It's not always easy to trust that our children will learn everything they need to know when they're ready. I sometimes wish I could go back in time and tell the younger me that everything will be all right! Just like every other unschooling parent, I've had my fears and doubts.

In those first years of unschooling, a phone call from one of my friends in Holland — whose children attended school — was enough to make me panic. When I heard about all of her children's school work, I sometimes worried that we were falling "behind schedule".

Unschooling is based on trust.

Unschooling is based on trust. But whenever I started worrying, I found it hard to hold on to that trust. Out of fear, I would set everyone at the table to practice writing and math. It wasn't that I didn't trust *them*, but that I didn't trust the process. What if I'd made the wrong decision? I was doing what my heart was telling me to do, but what if my heart was wrong? The real problem was that I didn't unschool when I was a child. I had never been trusted to learn naturally, to know intuitively what was right for me, so how could I have that kind of trust now?

I've had many moments like that one, especially when we first started unschooling. Each time, I had to overcome my fears and set my doubts aside to be able to trust freely again. While it wasn't always easy, it's been well worth the effort. Our trust in each other and in ourselves is now so strong that fear and worry hardly stand a chance.

It helped me to read about the experiences of other unschooling families and to discover like-minded friends through online and local support groups. But what helped most of all was the unconditional trust my children placed in me. "She'll be all right in a minute", I overheard Rutger tell Stijn at one of those moments. "Oh, yes, I know," Stijn answered, "she's just a bit scared right now." The moment he said that, my fear melted away. I realized that it didn't matter if my children learned on the same schedule as those of my friend. All that mattered was that we trusted them to learn on their own schedule. By meeting their needs and learning to trust, we have discovered to our delight that unschooling is simply living life, naturally and joyfully.

© 2001 Nanda Van Gestel

A Mother's Helper

Though housework is still pretty overwhelming for me, de-junking helps, and almost by mistake I've come across a real gold mine: a mother's helper. This is something I had thought about in the past but had never done anything about.

By chance I met a very eager 11-year-old girl who lives nearby. Today was her first day here. In five hours, Amy vacuumed, washed dishes (three times), folded laundry (twice), made granola, helped put things away, and played with Helen (2½). I was able to do several loads of laundry and hang them out, sweep and wash the kitchen floor, put away laundry, and do some proofreading for *Growing Without Schooling*. We both stopped working as necessary to be with the children, but Greta (3 mos.) was mostly happy to watch, and Helen was thrilled to have a new friend around.

Amy knows we can't afford to pay her very much, but is very excited to be earning some spending money. With the good start we got today I probably won't need her too often, but she's always welcome to come and play with the children.

Why I Chose Unschooling

by Kim Houssenloge

It all started when I first had my sweet, precious little bundle of joy. Three weeks prior to his birth I was a teacher in a state primary school. I enjoyed my job and thought that I'd return after my baby's birth, at some point. Once Lewi entered the world, however, my thoughts drastically changed. I couldn't imagine handing my precious little bundle over to anyone else. Surely no one could love him as I did?

From very early on I thought about Lewi's education. As time went on I realized that I couldn't just hand him over to any old school at the age of five.

By the time he was three, I started seriously thinking about where on earth I could send him to school. I looked into all of the local state schools and realized that I no longer had the same view of the education system that I'd had only a few years before. At this time I was also doing some private tutoring (which I'd been doing for years as a teacher). I felt the need to stop as I didn't really feel I could reach the kids I was trying to help. They improved in terms of the system's demands upon them but they weren't developing the love of learning and passion for knowledge that my three-year-old boy had. What was wrong? I wasn't sure at the time. I now know.

I looked into Montessori and its approach to learning. I found elements of this that appealed to me, and pursued this option. I visited the school, I went to its open days, I met the teachers, I questioned them all. Something didn't feel right there for me.

My search for the best school for Lewi continued. I started looking into homeschooling as an option. It felt good to me in many ways, but it was a relatively new concept. As a teacher, I felt homeschooling to be a strange choice for parents to make. (I take that all back now!) Due to the negative feedback I got whenever I mentioned my thoughts about possibly homeschooling Lewi, and also the amount of unanswered questions I had about the whole concept of not going to school, I put the idea aside and continued on my search for the right school.

By the time Lewi had turned four I was agonizing over whether or not to send him to preschool. In my heart it felt wrong, but all his friends were enrolling and he said he wanted to go. After many conversations with the staff at the local preschool, and due to my thoughts that he'd probably be going to school the following year anyway, I reluctantly sent him along. He loved it. He had lots of fun and developed a lovely bond with his teacher.

There was nothing in need of change.
He was already living life to the fullest.

At about the same time I began looking into the Waldorf Steiner philosophy for learning. I went to open days, I talked to teachers, I spoke to parents of children already at the school. I spoke to friends who were going to send their children there. I surfed the net looking for information. Although there were elements of the approach that I really liked, it was still a system of learning. It was a school situation with lots of children, where everyone had to do similar things at similar times every day — 6 hours a day, five days a week.

During my research into the Steiner approach, I began looking again into homeschooling as an option. It was then that I came upon unschooling and natural learning. I became intrigued by the philosophy that children learn best when they are given the freedom to choose their own learning for themselves. I learned more about the nature of learning in a few short months than I ever did as a student in the school system and later on as a university student.

Giving children the opportunities to self-direct their own learning and self-regulate their lives was a new concept to me. But looking at Lewi's life and realizing that he was learning all he needed to learn right then and there, regardless of a school system, felt empowering and wonderful. This is what I felt was missing in those years of my teaching career. No wonder students needed so many incentives and rewards to keep them going! They were learning, but they were learning what I wanted them to learn (or the Department of Education wanted them to learn). They weren't learning what was important to them. They were very rarely given the freedom of choice. They weren't able to dream and devise and hope and discuss their own paths. Their paths were chosen and that was that. The more I looked into natural learning, the more I loved it. This was what I'd been searching for. Lewi had been natural learning all of his little life. It felt right.

Looking at the results of natural learning in Lewi's first four years of life, I could see a passionate little boy who had an all-consuming thirst for knowledge and learning. He was a lover of books. A lover of nature. A fanatic about anything he was interested in at the time. He was motivated and self-directed and loved to play. There was nothing, the unschooling approach explained, in need of change. Nothing needed implementing. Nothing needed to happen to Lewi at the age of five for him to suddenly switch on to learning — he was already there, doing it, living life to the fullest.

I had finally reached the place that I needed to get to make the best decision for Lewi's education. So, after five days of preschool, I pulled him out. Much to my family and friends' surprise and some disapproval, I had made the absolute best, heart decision I'd ever made. It felt right. It felt normal. It felt peaceful for Lewi to just stay at home and not enter a system to be institutionalized, to stay at home and keep doing what we'd always done.

That year I read and read and read. I grabbed at anything to do with unschooling and natural learning. I joined discussion groups left right and center. I printed out reams and reams of fantastic articles on all sorts of related topics. I bought lots of good books form great authors on this approach to learning. I found John Holt and John Taylor Gatto. I learned about how children learn. I learned about how they fail. I learned the most I've ever learned about learning and the education system in that single year. I felt armed and ready.

By the time Lewi turned five, I knew I'd have some explaining to do. The questions poured in at me from all angles: Why would you choose to homeschool? Won't he get bored? What about social-ization? What about you, how will you get a break? How is he going to function normally? How will he make friends? How will he fit into society? Tell me you're not going to do this for the high school years? What about university — aren't you depriving him?

At the time I had some answers — now I think I have most of them. It was a daunting time. I felt a real lack of support. So I decided to make a concerted effort to find some like-minded people. I knew that both Lewi and I would need this type of support and social outlet in our lives. I phoned around searching for anyone in our local area who homeschooled. To my relief I found some. On making the initial contacts and attempting to get some get-togethers happening, however, it felt as though regular contact was not going to be possible. I started to feel despondent and concerned that we wouldn't have the support I'd really hoped for.

One day, this all changed for the better. On arriving home from an outing, there was a message on my answering machine. It was a local family trying to make contact with as many homeschoolers as possible. They wanted to homeschool and asked if we would all like to get together and meet to discuss homeschooling. We all turned out to be natural learners! Who would've thought? This was the beginning of a wonderful, wonderful group. We now meet once a month and have great raves about learning and our children. We also meet with other homeschoolers once a month and have fun outings together.

Life for us is great. No hurried mornings trying to get to school on time, no "I don't want to go to school" comments, no "I don't want to do homework", no bullying, no tired and cranky child at the end of the day (well, not most days at least). Our days are spent enjoying life. Lewi is free to choose whatever it is he'd like to do. There are no schedules to follow. No deadlines to meet. No changing of topics when he's right in the middle of something fun or important to him. No pushing him to do something he's finding too hard or boring. No having to stop when a bell rings. No having to ask to go to the toilet. No waiting to eat even when you're starving. No lining up. No hands up to talk. No staying in late. No detentions for talking in class — actually, talking is encouraged! Lots of time to play and dream; laugh and run; swim and ride; read and listen; and talk, talk, talk. He gets to experience real life with real people. He's learning to interact with the world safely and confidently and with room to grow and change in a natural way.

He loves his life and he loves learning.

He's learned to read and he's developing his writing. He loves most things to do with numbers. He's telling the time. He loves to draw, and paint and make things. He loves to construct and build. He's passionate about the natural world and the sciences. He's enthused about the history relevant to his interests. He's confident on the computer and can surf the Internet. He loves riding his bike and swimming and exploring. He likes to kick a ball around and have a game of cricket. He loves playing with his friends and having fun. He loves to be outside and explore nature. He loves delving into his imagination and making up fantastical stories, characters and worlds. He's doing all this freely and in a self-directed way. His learning is his own.

And when it all boils down, he's just a normal child doing normal things. He loves his life and he loves learning. He's happy and content. He loves this way of life. What more could anyone want for him?

© 2005 Kim Houssenloge

"It is nothing short of a miracle that the modern methods of instruction have not yet entirely strangled the holy curiosity of inquiry; for this delicate little plant, aside from stimulation, stands mainly in need of freedom; without this it goes to wrack and ruin without fail."

Albert Einstein

Schooling: The Hidden Agenda

by Daniel Quinn

A talk given at the Houston Unschoolers Group
Family Learning Conference, October 6 & 7, 2000.

I suspect that not everyone in this audience knows who I am or why I've been invited to speak to you today. After all, I've never written a book or even an article about homeschooling or unschooling. I've been called a number of things: a futurist, a planetary philosopher, an anthropologist from Mars. Recently I was introduced to an audience as a cultural critic, and I think this probably says it best. As you'll see, in my talk to you today, I will be trying to place schooling and unschooling in the larger context of our cultural history and that of our species as well.

For those of you who are unfamiliar with my work, I should begin by explaining what I mean by "our culture". Rather than burden you with a definition, I'll give you a simple test that you can use wherever you go in the world. If the food in that part of the world is under lock and key, and the people who live there have to work to get it, then you're among people of our culture. If you happen to be in a jungle in the interior of Brazil or New Guinea, however, you'll find that the food is not under lock and key. It's simply out there for the taking, and anyone who wants some can just go and get it. The people who live in these areas, often called aboriginals, stone-age peoples, or tribal peoples clearly belong to a culture radically different from our own.

I first began to focus my attention on the peculiarities of our own culture in the early 1960s, when I went to work for what was then a cutting-edge publisher of educational materials, Science Research Associates. I was in my mid-twenties and as thoroughly acculturated as any senator, bus driver, movie star, or medical doctor. My fundamental acceptances about the universe and humanity's place in it were rock-solid and thoroughly conventional.

41

But it was a stressful time to be alive, in some ways even more stressful than the present. Many people nowadays realize that human life may well be in jeopardy, but this jeopardy exists in some vaguely defined future, twenty or fifty or a hundred years hence. But in those coldest days of the Cold War everyone lived with the realization that a nuclear holocaust could occur literally at any second, without warning. It was very realistically the touch of a button away.

Human life would not be entirely snuffed out in a holocaust of this kind. In a way, it would be even worse than that. In a matter of hours, we would be thrown back not just to the Stone Age but to a level of almost total helplessness. In the Stone Age, after all, people lived perfectly well without supermarkets, shopping malls, hardware stores, and all the elaborate systems that keep these places stocked with the things we need. Within hours our cities would disintegrate into chaos and anarchy, and the necessities of life would vanish from store shelves, never to be replaced. Within days famine would be widespread.

Skills that are taken for granted among Stone Age peoples would be unknown to the survivors — the ability to differentiate between edible and inedible foods growing in their own environment, the ability to stalk, kill, dress, and preserve game animals, and most important the ability to make tools from available materials. How many of you know how to cure a hide? How to make a rope from scratch? How to flake a stone tool? Much less how to smelt metal from raw ore. Commonplace skills of the Paleolithic, developed over thousands of years, would be lost arts.

All this was freely acknowledged by people who didn't doubt for a moment that we were living the way humans were meant to live from the beginning of time, who didn't doubt for a moment that the things our children were learning in school were exactly the things they *should* be learning.

I'd been hired at SRA to work on a major new mathematics program that had been under development for several years in Cleveland. In my first year, we were going to publish the kindergarten and first-grade programs. In the second year, we'd publish the second-grade program, in the third year, the third-grade program, and so on. Working on the kindergarten and first-grade programs, I observed something that I thought was truly remarkable. In these grades, children spend most of their time learning things that no one growing up in our culture could possibly *avoid* learning. For example, they learn the names of the primary colors. Wow, just imagine missing school on the day when they were learning *blue*. You'd spend the rest of your life wondering what color the sky is. They learn to tell time, to count, and to add and subtract, as if anyone could possibly fail to learn these things in this culture. And of course they make the beginnings of learning how to read. I'll go out on a limb here and suggest an experiment. Two classes of 30 kids, taught identically and given the identical text materials throughout their school experience, but one class is given no instruction in reading at all and the other is given the usual instruction. Call it the Quinn Conjecture: both classes will test the same on reading skills at the end of twelve years. I feel safe in making this conjecture because ultimately kids learn to read the same way they learn to speak, by hanging around people who read and by wanting to be able to do what these people do.

Kids learn to read the same way they learn to speak.

It occurred to me at this time to ask this question: Instead of spending two or three years teaching children things they will inevitably learn anyway, why not teach them some things they will *not* inevitably learn and that they would actually *enjoy* learning at this age? How to navigate by the stars, for example. How to tan a hide. How to distinguish edible foods from inedible foods. How to build a shelter from scratch. How to make tools from scratch. How to make a canoe. How to track animals — all the forgotten but still valuable skills that our civilization is actually built on.

Of course I didn't have to vocalize this idea to anyone to know how it would be received. Being thoroughly acculturated, I could myself explain why it was totally inane. The way we live is the way humans were meant to live from the beginning of time, and our children were being prepared to enter that life. Those who came before us were savages, little more than brutes. Those who continue to live the way our ancestors lived are savages, little more than brutes. The world is well rid of them, and we're well rid of every vestige of them, including their ludicrously primitive skills.

Hundreds of ideas were implemented —
and still the schools failed.

Our children were being prepared in school to step boldly into the only fully human life that had ever existed on this planet. The skills they were acquiring in school would bring them not only success but deep personal fulfillment on every level. What did it matter if they never did more than work in some mind-numbing factory job? They could parse a sentence! They could explain to you the difference between a Petrarchan sonnet and a Shakespearean sonnet! They could extract a square root! They could show you why the square of the two sides of a right triangle were equal to the square of the hypotenuse! They could analyze a poem! They could explain to you how a bill passes congress! They could very possibly trace for you the economic causes of the Civil War. They had read Melville and Shakespeare, so why would they not now read Dostoevsky and Racine, Joyce and Beckett, Faulkner and O'Neill? But above all else, of course, the citizen's education — grades K to twelve — prepared children to be fully-functioning participants in this great civilization of ours. The day after their graduation exercises, they were ready to stride confidently toward any goal they might set themselves.

Of course, then, as now, everyone knew that the citizen's education was doing no such thing. It was perceived then — as now — that there was something strangely *wrong* with the schools. They were failing — and failing miserably — at delivering on these enticing promises. Ah well, teachers weren't being paid enough, so what could you expect? We raised teachers' salaries — again and again and again — and still the schools failed. Well, what could you expect? The schools were physically decrepit, lightless, and uninspiring. We built new ones — tens of thousands, hundreds of thousands of them — and still the schools failed. Well, what could you expect? The curriculum was antiquated and irrelevant. We modernized the curriculum, did our damnedest to make it relevant — and still the schools failed. Every week — then as now — you could read about some bright new idea that would surely "fix" whatever was wrong with our schools: the open classroom, team teaching, back to basics, more homework, less homework, no homework — I couldn't begin to enumerate them all. Hundreds of these bright ideas were implemented — thousands of them were implemented — and still the schools failed.

Within our cultural matrix, every medium tells us that the schools exist to prepare children for a successful and fulfilling life in our civilization (and are therefore failing). This is beyond argument, beyond doubt, beyond question. In *Ishmael* I said that the voice of Mother Culture speaks to us from every newspaper and magazine article, every movie, every sermon, every book, every parent, every teacher, every school administrator, and what she has to say about the schools is that they exist to prepare children for a successful and fulfilling life in our civilization (and are therefore failing). Once we step outside our cultural matrix, this voice no longer fills our ears and we're free to ask some new questions. Suppose the schools *aren't* failing? Suppose they're doing exactly what we *really* want them to do — but don't wish to examine and acknowledge?

Granted that the schools do a poor job of preparing children for a successful and fulfilling life in our civilization, but what things do they do excellently well? Well, to begin with, they do a superb job of keeping young people out of the job market. Instead of becoming wage-earners at age twelve or fourteen, they remain consumers only — and they consume billions of dollars worth of merchandise, using money that their parents earn. Just imagine what would happen to our economy if overnight the high schools closed their doors. Instead of having fifty million active consumers out there, we would suddenly have fifty million unemployed youth. It would be nothing short of an economic catastrophe.

Of course the situation was very different two hundred years ago, when we were still a primarily agrarian society. Youngsters were expected and needed to become workers at age ten, eleven, and twelve. For the masses, a fourth, fifth, or sixth-grade education was deemed perfectly adequate. But as the character of our society changed, fewer youngsters were needed for farm work, and the enactment of child-labor laws soon made it impossible to put ten-, eleven-, and twelve-year-olds to work in factories. It was necessary to keep them off the streets — and where better than in schools? Naturally, new material had to be inserted into the curriculum to fill up the time. It didn't much matter what it was. Have them memorize the capitals of every state. Have them memorize the principle products of every state. Have them learn the steps a bill takes in passing Congress. No one wondered or cared if these were things kids wanted to know or needed to know — or would *ever* need to know. No one wondered or ever troubled to find out if the material being added to the curriculum was retained. The educators didn't *want* to know, and, really, what difference would it make? It didn't matter that, once learned, they were immediately forgotten. It filled up some time. The law decreed that an eighth-grade education was essential for every citizen, and so curriculum writers provided material needed for an eighth-grade education.

During the Great Depression it became urgently important to keep young people off the job market for as long as possible, and so it came to be understood that a twelfth-grade education was essential for every citizen. As before, it didn't much matter what was added to fill up the time, so long as it was marginally plausible. Let's have them learn how to analyze a poem, even if they never read another one in their whole adult life. Let's have them read a great classic novel, even if they never read another one in their whole adult life. Let's have them study world history, even if it all just goes in one ear and out the other. Let's have them study Euclidean geometry, even if two years later they couldn't prove a single theorem to save their lives. All these things and many, many more were of course justified on the basis that they would contribute to the success and rich fulfillment that these children would experience as adults. Except, of course, that it didn't. But no one wanted to know about that. No one would have dreamed of testing young people five years after graduation to find out how much of it they'd retained. No one would have dreamed of asking them how useful it had been to them in realistic terms or how much it had contributed to their success and fulfillment as humans. What would be the point of asking *them* to evaluate their education? What did *they* know about it, after all? They were just high school graduates, not professional educators.

At the end of the Second World War, no one knew what the economic future was going to be like. With the disappearance of the war industries, would the country fall back into the pre-war depression slump? The word began to go out that the citizen's education should really include four years of college. *Everyone* should go to college. As the economy continued to grow, however, this injunction began to be softened. Four years of college would sure be good for you, but it wasn't part of the citizen's education, which ultimately remained a twelfth-grade education.

The curriculum had achieved the status of scripture.

It was in the good years following the war, when there were often more jobs than workers to fill them, that our schools began to be perceived as failing. With ready workers in demand, it was apparent that kids were coming out of school without knowing much more than the sixth-grade graduates of a century ago. They'd "gone through" all the material that had been added to fill up the time — analyzed poetry, diagramed sentences, proved theorems, solved for *x*, plowed through thousands of pages of history and literature, written bushels of themes, but for the most part they retained almost none of it —

and of how much use would it be to them if they had? From a business point of view, these high-school graduates were barely employable.

But of course by then the curriculum had achieved the status of scripture, and it was too late to acknowledge that the program had never been designed to be *useful.* The educators' response to the business community was, "We just have to give the kids more of the same — more poems to analyze, more sentences to diagram, more theorems to prove, more equations to solve, more pages of history and literature to read, more themes to write, and so on." No one was about to acknowledge that the program had been set up to keep young people off the job market — and that it had done a damn fine job of *that* at least.

Children are the most fantastic learners in the world.

But keeping young people off the job market is only half of what the schools do superbly well. By the age of thirteen or fourteen, children in aboriginal societies — tribal societies — have completed what we, from our point of view, would call their "education". They're ready to "graduate" and become adults. In these societies, what this means is that their survival value is 100%. All their elders could disappear overnight, and there wouldn't be chaos, anarchy, and famine among these new adults. They would be able to carry on without a hitch. None of the skills and technologies practiced by their parents would be lost. If they wanted to, they could live quite independently of the tribal structure in which they were reared.

But the last thing we want our children to be able to do is to live independently of our society. We don't want our graduates to have a survival value of 100%, because this would make them free to opt out of our carefully constructed economic system and do whatever they please. We don't want them to do whatever they please, we want them to have exactly two choices (assuming they're not independently wealthy). Get a job or go to college. Either choice is good for us, because we need a constant supply of entry-level workers and we also need doctors, lawyers, physicists, mathematicians, psychologists, geologists, biologists, school teachers, and so on. The citizen's education accomplishes this almost without fail. Ninety-nine point nine percent of our high school graduates make one of these two choices.

And it should be noted that our high-school graduates are reliably *entry-level* workers. We want them to *have* to grab the lowest rung on the ladder. What sense would it make to give them skills that would make it possible for them to grab the second rung or the third rung? Those are the rungs their older brothers and sisters are reaching for. And if this year's graduates were reaching for the second or third rungs, who would be doing the work at the bottom? The business people who do the hiring constantly complain that graduates know absolutely nothing, have virtually no useful skills at all. But in truth how could it be otherwise?

So you see that our schools are not failing, they're just succeeding in ways we prefer not to see. Turning out graduates with no skills, with no survival value, and with no choice but to work or starve are not *flaws* of the system, they are *features* of the system. These are the things the system *must do* to keep things going on as they are.

Our schools are not failing, they're just succeeding in ways we prefer not to see.

The need for schooling is bolstered by two well-entrenched pieces of cultural mythology. The first and most pernicious of these is that children *will not learn* unless they're compelled to — in school. It is part of the mythology of childhood itself that children *hate* learning and will avoid it at all costs. Of course, anyone who has had a child knows what an absurd lie this is. From infancy onward, children are the most fantastic learners in the world. If they grow up in a family in which four languages are spoken, they will be speaking four languages by the time they're three or four years old — without a day of schooling, just by hanging around the members of their family, because they desperately want to be able to do the things they do. Anyone who has had a child knows that they are tirelessly curious. As soon as they're *able* to ask questions, they ask questions incessantly, often driving their parents to distraction. Their curiosity extends to everything they can reach, which is why every parent soon learns to put anything breakable, anything dangerous, anything untouchable up high — and if possible behind lock and key. We all know the truth of the joke about those childproof bottle caps: those are the kind that only children can open.

The desire to learn is hardwired into the human child.

People who imagine that children are resistant to learning have a nonexistent understanding of how human culture developed in the first place. Culture is no more and no less than the totality of *learned* behavior and information that is passed from one generation to the next. The desire to eat is not transmitted by culture, but knowledge about how edible foods are found, collected, and processed *is* transmitted by culture. Before the invention of writing, whatever was not passed on from one generation to the next was simply lost, no matter what it was — a technique, a song, a detail of history. Among aboriginal peoples — those we haven't destroyed — the transmission between generations is remarkably complete, but of course not 100% complete. There will always be trivial details of personal history that the older generation takes to its grave. But the vital material is never lost.

This comes about because the desire to learn is *hardwired* into the human child just the way that the desire to reproduce is hardwired into the human adult. It's genetic. If there was ever a strain of humans whose children were *not* driven to learn, they're long gone, because they *could not be* culture-bearers.

Children don't have to be *motivated* to learn everything they can about the world they inhabit, they're absolutely *driven* to learn it. By the onset of puberty, children in aboriginal societies have unfailingly learned everything they need to function as adults.

Think of it this way. In the most general terms, the human biological clock is set for two alarms. When the first alarm goes off, at birth, the clock chimes *learn, learn, learn, learn, learn.* When the second alarm goes off, at the onset of puberty, the clock chimes *mate, mate, mate, mate, mate.* The chime that goes *learn, learn, learn* never disappears entirely, but it becomes relatively faint at the onset of puberty. At that point, children cease to want to follow their parents around in the learning dance. Instead, they want to follow *each other* around in the mating dance.

We, of course, in our greater wisdom have decreed that the biological clock regulated by our genes must be ignored.

They're convinced that children don't want to learn anything at all — and they point to school children to prove it.

What sells most people on the idea of school is the fact that the unschooled child learns what it *wants* to learn *when* it wants to learn it. This is intolerable to them, because they're convinced that children don't want to learn anything at all — and they point to school children to prove it. What they fail to recognize is that the learning curve of preschool children swoops upward like a mountain — but quickly levels off when they enter school. By the third or fourth grade it's completely flat for most kids. Learning, such as it is, has become a boring, painful experience they'd love to be able to avoid if they could. But there's another reason why people abhor the idea of children learning what they want to learn when they want to learn it. *They won't all learn the same things!* Some of them will never learn to analyze a poem! Some of them will never learn to parse a sentence or write a theme! Some of them will never read *Julius Caesar!* Some will never learn geometry! Some will never dissect a frog! Some will never learn how a bill passes Congress! Well, of course, this is too horrible to imagine. It doesn't matter that 90% of these students will never read another poem or another play by Shakespeare in their lives. It doesn't matter that 90% of them will never have occasion to parse another sentence or write another theme in their lives. It doesn't matter that 90% retain no functional knowledge of the geometry or algebra they studied. It doesn't matter that 90% never have any use for whatever knowledge they were supposed to gain from dissecting a frog. It doesn't matter that 90% graduate without having the vaguest idea how a bill passes Congress. All that matters is that they've *gone through it!*

People remember the things they need to know.

The people who are horrified by the idea of children learning what they want to learn when they want to learn it have not accepted the very elementary psychological fact that people (all people, of every age) remember the things that are important to them — the things they *need to know* — and forget the rest. I am a living witness to this fact. I went to one of the best prep schools in the country and graduated fourth in my class, and I doubt very much if I could now get a passing grade in more than two or three of the dozens of courses I took. I studied classical Greek for two solid years, and now would be unable to read aloud a single sentence.

One final argument people advance to support the idea that children *need* all the schooling we give them is that there is *vastly more material* to be learned today than there was in prehistoric times or even a century ago. Well, there is of course vastly more material that *can* be learned, but we all know perfectly well that it isn't being taught in grades K to twelve. Whole vast new fields of knowledge exist today — things no one even heard of a century ago: astrophysics, biochemistry, paleobiology, aeronautics, particle physics, ethology, cytopathology, neurophysiology — I could list them for hours. But are these the things that we have jammed into the K-12 curriculum because everyone needs to know them? Certainly not. The idea is absurd. The idea that children need to be schooled for a long time because there is so much that *can be* learned is absurd. If the citizen's education were to be extended to include everything that *can be* learned, it wouldn't run to grade twelve, it would run to grade twelve thousand, and no one would be able to graduate in a single lifetime.

I know of course that there is no one in this audience who needs to be sold on the virtues of homeschooling or unschooling. I hope, however, that I may have been able to add some philosophical, historical, anthropological, and biological foundation for your conviction that school ain't all it's cracked up to be.

© 2000 Daniel Quinn

"If I had to make a general rule for living and working with children, it might be this: be wary of saying or doing anything to a child that you would not do to another adult, whose good opinion and affection you valued."

John Holt

How Do We Know
They're Learning?

by Jan Hunt

In unschooling, the child's current interests are followed, and the parents act not as teachers but as tutors and resource assistants. This approach is often misunderstood, because it is based on assumptions that are quite different from those implicit in conventional schooling.

Unschoolers are often described by what we do *not* do; we do not "teach"; we do not impose an arbitrary, artificial curriculum; we do not structure the hours of our "school day". But there are so many things we do:

- Answer questions. Many of us believe that this is the most essential aspect of unschooling.

- Encourage creative and cooperative solutions to problems as they arise.

- Find resources and information to support whatever interests the child is currently exploring.

- Attempt to illustrate, through the daily decisions we make, the benefits of such personal moral qualities as friendship, honesty, and responsibility.

- Model the joy of learning through our own discussions, reading, and research.

While it is not impossible for a conventionally schooling family to pursue the kinds of activities I have described, it is simply more difficult to do so when parents and children have so much less time together, and when even after-school hours are taken up by projects, homework, and other school-related demands. School children can also become used to seeking emotional support from peers rather than parents, and this pattern can be difficult to interrupt even when school is not in session.

The assumption that unschooling parents somehow lack awareness of their children's progress, and therefore require formal evaluation of that progress, is related to the fact that unschoolers function outside the arena of the schools, and our philosophies and methods are not always well-understood.

How do unschooling parents know their children are learning? The answer to this question is, to put it most simply, direct observation. I have only one child. If a teacher had only one child in her classroom, and was unable to describe the reading skills of that child, everyone would be dismayed — how could a teacher have such close daily contact with one child and miss something so obvious? Yet many people unfamiliar with unschooling imagine that parents with just this sort of close daily contact with their child require outside evaluation to determine that child's progress. This puzzles unschooling parents, who cannot imagine missing anything so interesting as the nature of their child's learning.

No unschooling parents have twenty-five children, and we are thus free to focus on the enhancement of learning without being continually distracted by the many time-consuming tasks, unrelated to learning, that are necessary in a classroom situation. This freedom from distraction is a major factor in the establishment of a lively, creative, and joyful learning environment.

Any parent of a toddler could almost certainly tell us how many numbers her child can count to, and how many colors he knows — not through testing, but simply through many hours of listening to his questions and statements. In unschooling, this type of observation simply continues on into higher ages and more complex learning.

There are many times in the course of a day when a reasonably curious child will want to know the meaning of certain printed words

— in books and newspapers, on the computer or television, on board game instruction cards, on package labels, on mail that has just arrived, and so on. If this child's self-esteem is intact, he will not hesitate to ask his parents the meaning of these words. Through the decrease of questions of this type, and the actual reading aloud of certain words, ("Look, Daddy, this package is for you!") it seems safe to assume that reading is progressing in the direction of literacy. This may seem to outsiders to be somewhat imprecise, but unschooling parents learn through experience that more specific evaluation is intrusive, unnecessary, and self-defeating.

Specific evaluation is intrusive,
unnecessary, and self-defeating.

If the government were to establish compulsory evaluation of babies to determine whether they were walking on schedule, everyone would think that was absurd. We all know that healthy babies walk eventually, and that it would be futile and frustrating to attempt to speed up that process — as foolish as trying to speed up the blooming of a rose. Gardeners do not worry about late-blooming roses, or measure their daily progress — they trust in nature's good intentions, meet the needs of the plants under their care, and know that any further intervention would interfere with the natural flow of their growth. Such trust is as essential in the education of a child as it is in gardening. All healthy rose bushes bloom when ready, all healthy babies walk when ready, and all healthy children in a family of readers read when ready — though this may be as late as ten or twelve. There is no need to speed up or measure this process. When a child is free to learn at his own pace, he will continue to love learning throughout his life.

The child's progress is not always smooth; there may be sudden shifts from one stage to the next. Formal evaluation given just prior to such a shift may give unfair and misleading information. At a time when I knew (through a reduction in the number of requests for me to read certain signs, labels, etc.) that my son Jason's reading was improving, but not, as far as I knew, able to read fluently, I told him one evening that I was unable to read to him because I wasn't feeling well. He said, "Well, you can rest and I'll read a book to you." He proceeded to read an entire book flawlessly, at a level of more difficulty than I would have guessed.

A schedule of intellectual growth exists within each child.

Thus it sometimes happens in the natural course of living with a child that we receive direct and specific information about his progress. But it should be stressed that this is part of the natural process of supporting a child's learning, and that requiring such direct proof is almost always self-defeating. Had I required him to read the book, he might well have refused, because he would have felt the anxiety which anyone feels when being evaluated. But because he chose to read voluntarily, and his accuracy was not being examined, he had no reason to feel anxious.

Unschooling parents, then, cannot avoid having a good general idea of a child's progress in reading, or in any other area. Without testing for specific learning, we may underestimate a child's abilities to some extent, but all that means is that we make delightful discoveries along the way.

If unschooling parents do not measure, evaluate and control learning, how can the child himself know when to move on to the next level? If we were to ask a horticulturist how a rose knows when to bloom, he or she could not answer that question; it is simply assumed that such knowledge is built into the wondrous genetics of the seed. A child's schedule of intellectual growth, like the rose's blooming, may indeed be a mysterious process, but it nonetheless exists within each child.

Jason, one day at age three, though not yet a fluent reader, taught himself squares and square roots. How could I have guessed that he was ready for that level of mathematics on that particular day? Had I been imposing a standard curriculum, I might have discouraged early math and emphasized reading, and to what end? He is now proficient in, and greatly enjoys, both areas. Ultimately, it made no difference when he achieved this mastery. As John Holt once observed, children are not trains. If a train does not reach every station on time, it will be late reaching its ultimate destination. But a child can be late at any "station", and can even change the entire route of the learning process, and still reach every area of learning.

The unschooling child not only knows what he needs to learn, but how best to go about learning it. Jason has always devised ingenious ways for learning what is currently in the foreground of his interest. His method for learning squares and square roots — rows and columns of dots on paper — would never have occurred to me, even if I had guessed correctly that he was ready for this subject at that early age. At age 6, he was looking over a new globe, and made a game of guessing which of several pairs of countries was larger in area, then larger in population, and so on. These sorts of games went on constantly; his creativity in designing interesting learning methods far surpassed my own, and I never had to give a single thought to motivation. My child is not unique; many unschooling parents have reported just this sort of creativity and joyful learning in their children.

My role has not been that
of teacher, but of facilitator.

Jason has had no lessons in the conventional sense. He has taught himself, with help as needed and requested by him, reading, writing, math, art and science. However, these subjects are not treated as separate categories, but as parts of the topic of current interest. My role has not been that of teacher, but of facilitator. I am not merely a passive observer, however. When he asked questions — which he did many times each day, I answered as well as I could. If I couldn't, I became a researcher: I made phone calls, helped him to use the encyclopedia, went with him to the library, or found someone with relevant experience with whom he could learn; whatever helped him to find the answer (today's parents, of course, have the Internet as another resource). This was not merely helpful in answering his specific question, but in the more general sense of modeling the many ways in which information can be obtained.

If a child learns how to obtain information, he can apply that skill throughout his life.

While I did not choose unschooling for religious reasons, I have always welcomed the time available to explore questions of personal ethics, and to encourage such qualities as kindness, honesty, trust, cooperation, creative solutions to problems, and compassion for others. We have also appreciated having time in the morning to discuss such things as dreams from the previous night and plans for the day ahead, when I would otherwise have been preoccupied with helping him to get ready for school. Believing that modern life is already overly hectic, we try as much as possible to make room for unhurried time in our family.

In an age of "information explosion", it is no longer meaningful or realistic to require rote memorization of specific facts. Not only are these facts meaningless to the child unless they happen to coincide with his own current and unique interests, many of these facts will in any case be outdated by the time he is an adult. But if a child learns how to obtain information, he can apply that skill throughout his life. Regardless of which specific topics were covered, our primary focus has always been "how to learn" and "how to obtain information". As John Holt wrote, "Since we can't know what knowledge will be most needed in the future, it is senseless to try to teach it in advance. Instead, we should try to turn out people who love learning so much and learn so well that they will be able to learn whatever needs to be learned."

Asking About Numbers

Helen (6) asks a great many multiplication questions: "How much is 6 sixes?" for example. She also asks about addition and subtraction, and recently she realized that the more closely she herself is involved, the more easily she understands things — she figures out more easily how old she will be when her baby sister Alice is five than how old her other sister, Greta, will be, for example.

She knows a lot of numbers. For example, she seems really to *know* 6: that 2 + 4 = 6, 2 × 3 = 6, 6 − 1 = 5, etc. — all of those "number facts" that relate to 6. She has also shown a great interest in fractions. And for a while her favorite number was a hundred million: "How far is 100,000,000 inches?" "How long would it take to count to 100,000,000?" "Are there 100,000,000 people?" We get out the calculator and tell her how far 100,000,000 inches is (halfway from here to California), and whatever else we can tell her about what she wants to know.

Helen has also estimated amounts, 8 × 13, for example. She asked, "How much is 8 thirteens? About a hundred, I think." She has also estimated length, with ribbon, quite accurately. We never have lessons in arithmetic — or anything else — we answer questions.

What is Unschooling?

by Earl Stevens

"What we want to see is the child in pursuit of knowledge,
not knowledge in pursuit of the child."

– George Bernard Shaw

It is very satisfying for parents to see their children in pursuit of knowledge. It is natural and healthy for the children, and in the first few years of life, the pursuit goes on during every waking hour. But after a few short years, most kids go to school. The schools also want to see children in pursuit of knowledge, but the schools want them to pursue mainly the *school's* knowledge and devote twelve years of life to doing so.

In his acceptance speech for the New York City Teacher of the Year award (1990), John Gatto said, "Schools were designed by Horace Mann ... and others to be instruments of the scientific management of a mass population." In the interests of managing each generation of children, the public school curriculum has become a hopelessly flawed attempt to define education and to find a way of delivering that definition to vast numbers of children.

The traditional curriculum is based on the assumption that children must be pursued by knowledge because they will never pursue it themselves. It was no doubt noticed that, when given a choice, most children prefer not to do school work. Since, in a school, knowledge is *defined as schoolwork*, it is easy for educators to conclude that children don't like to acquire knowledge. Thus schooling came to be a method of controlling children and forcing them to do whatever educators decided was beneficial for them. Most children don't like textbooks, workbooks, quizzes, rote memorization, subject schedules, and lengthy periods of physical inactivity. One can discover this — even with polite and cooperative children — by asking them if they would like to add more time to their daily schedule. I feel certain that most will decline the offer.

The work of a schoolteacher is not the same as that of a home-schooling parent. In most schools, a teacher is hired to deliver a ready-made, standardized, year-long curriculum to 25 or more age-segregated children who are confined in a building all day. The teacher must use a standard curriculum — not because it is the best approach for encouraging an individual child to learn the things that need to be known — but because it is a convenient way to handle and track large numbers of children. The school curriculum is understandable only in the context of bringing administrative order out of daily chaos, of giving direction to frustrated children and unpredictable teachers. It is a system that staggers ever onward but never upward, and every morning we read about the results in our newspapers.

But despite the differences between the school environment and the home, many parents begin homeschooling under the impression that it can be pursued only by following some variation of the traditional public school curriculum in the home. Preoccupied with the idea of "equivalent education", state and local education officials assume that we must share their educational goals and that we home-school simply because we don't want our children to be inside their buildings. Textbook and curriculum publishing companies go to great lengths to assure us that we must buy their products if we expect our children to be properly educated. As if this were not enough, there are national, state, and local support organizations that have practically adopted the use of the traditional curriculum and the school-in-the-home image of homeschooling as a de facto member-ship requirement. In the midst of all this, it can be difficult for a new homeschooling family to think that an alternative approach is possible.

One alternative approach is unschooling, also known as natural learning, experience-based learning, or independent learning. When our local homeschooling support group announced a gathering to discuss unschooling, we thought a dozen or so people might attend, but more than 100 adults and children showed up. For three hours, parents and some of the children took turns talking about their homeschooling experiences and about unschooling. Many people said afterward that they left the meeting feeling reinforced and exhilarated — not because anybody told them what to do or gave them a magic formula — but because they grew more secure in making these decisions for themselves. Sharing ideas about this topic left them feeling empowered.

Unschooling isn't a method, it is a way of looking at children and at life.

Before I talk about what I think unschooling is, I must talk about what it isn't. Unschooling isn't a recipe, and therefore it can't be explained in recipe terms. It is impossible to give unschooling directions for people to follow so that it can be tried for a week or so to see if it works. Unschooling isn't a method, it is a way of looking at children and at life. It is based on trust that parents and children will find the paths that work best for them — without depending on educational institutions, publishing companies, or experts to tell them what to do.

Unschooling does not mean that parents can never teach anything to their children, or that children should learn about life entirely on their own without the help and guidance of their parents. Unschooling does not mean that parents give up active participation in the education and development of their children and simply hope that something good will happen. Finally, since many unschooling families have definite plans for college, unschooling does not even mean that children will never take a course in any kind of a school.

Then what is unschooling? I can't speak for every person who uses the term, but I can talk about my own experiences. Our son has never had an academic lesson, has never been told to read or to learn mathematics, science, or history. Nobody has told him about phonics. He has never taken a test or been asked to study or memorize anything. When people ask, "What do you do?" My answer is that we follow our interests — and our interests inevitably lead to science, literature, history, mathematics, music — all the things that have interested people before anybody thought of them as "subjects".

Unschooling children do real things all day long.

A large component of unschooling is grounded in doing real things, not because we hope they will be good for us, but because they are intrinsically fascinating. There is an energy that comes from this that you can't buy with a curriculum. Children do real things all day long, and in a trusting and supportive home environment, "doing real things" invariably brings about healthy mental development and valuable knowledge. It is natural for children to read, write, play with numbers, learn about society, find out about the past, think, wonder and do all those things that society so unsuccessfully attempts to force upon them in the context of schooling.

While few of us get out of bed in the morning in the mood for a "learning experience", I hope that all of us get up feeling in the mood for life. Children always do so — unless they are ill or life has been made overly stressful or confusing for them. Sometimes the problem for the parent is that it can be difficult to determine if anything important is actually going on. It is a little like watching a garden grow. No matter how closely we examine the garden, it is difficult to verify that anything is happening at that particular moment. But as the season progresses, we can see that much has happened, quietly and naturally. Children pursue life, and in doing so, pursue knowledge. They need adults to trust in the inevitability of this very natural process, and to offer what assistance they can.

Parents come to our unschooling discussions with many questions about fulfilling state requirements. They ask: "How do unschoolers explain themselves to the state when they fill out the paperwork every year?", "If you don't use a curriculum, what do you say?" and "What about required record-keeping?" To my knowledge, un-schoolers have had no problems with our state department of education over matters of this kind. This is a time when even many public school educators are moving away from the traditional curriculum, and are seeking alternatives to fragmented learning and drudgery.

Children pursue life, and in doing so, pursue knowledge.

When I fill out the paperwork required for homeschooling in our state, I briefly describe, in the space provided, what we are currently doing, and the general intent of what we plan to do for the coming year. I don't include long lists of books or describe any of the step-by-step skills associated with a curriculum. For example, under English and Language Arts, I mentioned that our son's favorite "subject" is the English language. I said a few words about our family library. I mentioned that our son reads a great deal and uses our computer for whatever writing he happens to do. I concluded that, "Since he already does so well on his own, we have decided not to introduce language skills as a subject to be studied. It seems to make more sense for us to leave him to his own continuing success."

Unschooling is a unique opportunity for each family to do whatever makes sense for the growth and development of their children. If we have a reason for using a curriculum and traditional school materials, we are free to use them. They are not a universally necessary or required component of unschooling, either educationally or legally.

Allowing curriculums, textbooks, and tests to be the defining, driving force behind the education of a child is a hindrance in the home as much as in the school — not only because it interferes with learning, but because it interferes with trust. As I have mentioned, even educators are beginning to question the pre-planned, year-long curriculum as an out-dated, 19th century educational system. There is no reason that families should be less flexible and innovative than schools.

Anne Sullivan, Helen Keller's mentor and friend, said:

"I am beginning to suspect all elaborate and special systems of education. They seem to me to be built up on the supposition that every child is a kind of idiot who must be taught to think. Whereas, if the child is left to himself, he will think more and better, if less showily. Let him go and come freely, let him touch real things and combine his impressions for himself, instead of sitting indoors at a little round table, while a sweet-voiced teacher suggests that he build a stone wall with his wooden blocks, or make a rainbow out of strips of coloured paper, or plant straw trees in bead flower-pots. Such teaching fills the mind with artificial associations that must be got rid of, before the child can develop independent ideas out of actual experiences." (Helen Keller, *The Story of My Life*, 1902)

Unschooling provides a unique opportunity to step away from systems and methods, and to develop independent ideas out of actual experiences, where the child is truly in pursuit of knowledge, not the other way around.

"Play is the highest form of research."

Albert Einstein

Learning Through Play

by Jan Hunt

My son Jason, now a young adult, has been unschooled from the beginning. We were fortunate to have discovered John Holt's books when Jason was two, and never looked back.

Jason was a very inquisitive child, who loved learning new words and playing with numbers. He had an extensive vocabulary by 18 months, understood the concept of infinity at 2, and taught himself squares and square roots at 3. In spite of all this, I still wondered if I should use a curriculum, especially for math. It was hard not to worry when taking a path that was so different from the one I had taken in childhood. It was also hard not to be affected by my parents' doubts, even though I understood the reasons for their skepticism.

When Jason was 7, he asked for a math book as his special holiday gift that year, after we read John Holt's glowing review of Harold Jacobs' book *Mathematics: A Human Endeavor*, in *Growing Without Schooling*. The book proved to be as wonderful as Holt had said, and we enjoyed it a lot. But a few months later, I noticed that Jason hadn't looked at it for a while. I decided to suggest reading a chapter per week together. Fortunately, I was busy that day and didn't get around to asking him. That evening, Jason came up to me, book in hand, saying "Let's play math." My first thought was, "Whew, that was a close one." Had I made my offer, he probably would have accepted it, and even learned from it, but where would the concept of *math as play* have gone?

When Jason was 8, my neighbor, who also had an 8-year-old son, asked me if Jason knew the times tables, and when I said he did, she asked me how he had learned it. Her son had struggled for months, and still had trouble remembering the answers. He was frustrated and worried about his grades, but none of her ideas had helped. I explained that Jason learned everything in a very natural way, as needed. For example, his dad had brought home a dart board, just for fun, a few months back. Scoring a darts game involves both addition and multiplication, and because Jason wanted to be the scorekeeper, he learned all the number combinations used for darts (and later learned other combinations as he needed them), though the dartboard had not been purchased with that in mind, nor had we ever used the term "times tables".

Unschooling isn't a technique; it's living and learning naturally, lovingly, and respectfully together.

Now, Jason can do math in his head, unlike me. Having memorized formulas, I can solve most math problems, but always on paper, and I rarely understand the concepts involved. Jason can not only do the math easily but really understands the whole process. If he happens to need a new mathematical tool, he can easily learn it. He needed to know about sines and cosines when he converted paintings into graphics for my children's book *A Gift for Baby*. He learned this quickly and easily from the Internet. I could only look back and remember how much time I had spent memorizing calculus formulas, and though I passed all the tests, I really hadn't learned anything. I didn't understand how the formulas actually worked, or how to use them in the real world.

Jason has learned much of what he knows through play, and has the same love of learning he was born with. He learned about money by playing Monopoly, about spelling by playing Scrabble, about strategies by playing chess, Clue, and video games, about our culture by watching classic and modern TV shows and films, about politics and government by watching "Yes, Minister", about grammar by playing Mad Libs, about fractions by cooking, about words by playing Dictionary, and writing skills by reading P. G. Wodehouse.

He learns about life through living it. But all of this learning has taken place more incidentally than intentionally, as part of the larger business of living life freely and naturally.

During a recent newspaper interview for an article on unschooling, the reporter asked me which techniques unschoolers use that could be used by parents of children in school. I explained that unschooling isn't a technique; it's living and learning naturally, lovingly, and respectfully together. As my friend and unschooling parent Mary Van Doren once wrote:

> "Raising children with an emphasis on intrinsic rewards is not a technique, a method or a trick to get them to do what the parent wants them to by subtler means, but a way of life, a way of living with children with real respect for their intelligence and for their being."

I feel indebted to John Holt and other unschooling writers for encouraging me to trust Jason to know what he needed and wanted to learn and how to go about learning it. But my best teacher has always been my son. For parents who went to school, unschooling can be a challenge, but it is also our best opportunity to learn to trust our children's natural love of learning.

Telling Stories

We did some camping this past summer, and decided not to bring books. Between nightfall and sleep, Helen (3) wanted to be read to — not possible. So we thought about telling stories, but no stories came to mind. How could that be? We quickly found a jumping-off point: we were camping, so Mark told us about camping as a Boy Scout.

Now we know we can always have relevant stories at any time. Helen loves to hear about Mama and Papa when they were children. She also likes to hear about herself when she was a baby and even what we did yesterday. I think as we go along we may start making up some stories too. We have enjoyed this a lot, though we certainly lacked confidence at first — the written word is so powerful in our lives.

What About College?

by Rue Kream

"School was the unhappiest time of my life and the worst trick it ever played on me was to pretend that it was the world in miniature. For it hindered me from discovering how lovely and delightful and kind the world can be, and how much of it is intelligible."

— E. M. Forester

Don't you worry that your kids will be unprepared when the time comes for them to leave the nest? What about college? I don't see how my kids will be prepared for the real world if they don't go to school, and I can't imagine dealing with a teenager at home all the time.

Our goal is that there will not be a particular moment when our children must suddenly be pushed from the nest. Our hope is that, by allowing our children to seek out and take responsibility in their own time with our guidance and support, but not pressure, they will experience a smoother transition into adulthood and will think of us as a safety net rather than an obstacle.

The problems of a typical teen/parent relationship are created in large part by the dynamics inherent in a system that separates parents and children from the time the child turns five years old (or often earlier). It is very difficult to retain a connected relationship when the amount of time spent together is so minimal and is so often spent in preparation for the next day's tasks. Add to that the fact that a mainstream teenager has little to no control over her own life or time, has little opportunity to pursue what interests her, is dealing with the flood of emotions that hormones bring, is put on a schedule that does not permit her the sleep her body needs, and lives in a society that encourages her to pull away from her parents at a certain age whether she wants to or not, and you have a recipe for unhappiness.

Our society has choreographed a "typical" progression from child to adult, and expects all teenagers to travel the same path. A person who doesn't feel comfortable on that path is a rebel or a delinquent. A child who is not ready to move on as quickly as another child might be is perceived as immature or spoiled or "slow". A child who is ready to move on more quickly than others has no opportunity to do so. Unschooling gives each child the time and the room to follow her own path and to travel that path with the loving support and companionship of her family.

The groundwork we lay with our kids when they are young is vitally important to our future relationships. The relationships I have with Dagny and Rowan are open, honest, and respectful. We have our difficult moments, just as anyone in a relationship does, but overall it's a pleasure to spend time with them. I have no reason to believe that will change at any particular "teen" age. We will ride the swells of hormones and growing pains together, and each of them will leave the nest in her own time and way.

I do not worry that they will be unprepared, because I trust that they will know when the time is right. They will have spent a lifetime making their own decisions about what they are capable of. Just as they knew when they were ready to tie their shoes, take off their training wheels, or watch a scary movie, they will know when they are ready to fly. They aren't in preparation for anything. They live in the real world right now, and it is a wonderful, amazing, challenging, beautiful, extraordinary place.

In *Teach Your Own*, John Holt wrote, "I used to say, and say now, that a college degree isn't a magic passkey that opens every door in town. It opens only a few, and before you spend a lot of time and money getting one of those keys, it's a good idea to find out what doors it opens (if any), and what's on the other side of those doors, and to decide whether you like what's on the other side, and if you do, whether there may not be an easier way to get there." Rowan and Dagny will decide for themselves whether college is the way to get where they want to go.

When people say that school prepares children for the real world, what's implied is that it is the difficult parts of school (doing things you don't want to do, forced interaction with peers, following rules that you don't believe in) that are important. What's implied is that the real world is going to be an unhappy place and that being treated unfairly by people is a part of life.

The real world
is what we make it.

It may be a part of life in school, but it is not a part of our lives. School is as far away from the real world as possible. In school we learn that we cannot control our own destinies and that it is acceptable to let others govern our lives. In the real world we can take responsibility for choosing our own paths and governing our own lives. The real world is what we make it. As unschoolers we can choose to make it fascinating and loving and peaceful, and we can immerse ourselves in it every day.

I believe that having your time regulated by bells, eating on a schedule, having very little privacy or opportunity for self-determination, having to ask permission to perform bodily functions, and having to think on command, causes nothing but a feeling of fear when you are finally let loose into the world. It does nothing to help you to live a joyful life.

No adult is forced to sit when she wants to run, listen when she wants to sing, draw when she wants to read, or be inside when she wants to be outside. The real lessons that children learn in school do nothing to improve their lives as adults and do much to hinder a joyful childhood. In *The Six-Lesson Schoolteacher*, John Taylor Gatto (New York City Teacher of the Year in 1990) lists the six lessons he believes are really taught in school:

- "The first lesson I teach is: 'Stay in the class where you belong.' I don't know who decides that my kids belong there but that's not my business."

- "The second lesson I teach kids is to turn on and off like a light switch."

- "The third lesson I teach you is to surrender your will to a predestined chain of command. Rights may be granted or withheld, by authority, without appeal. As a schoolteacher I intervene in many personal decisions, issuing a Pass for those I deem legitimate, or initiating a disciplinary confrontation for behavior that threatens my control."

- "The fourth lesson I teach is that only I determine what curriculum you will study. (Rather, I enforce decisions transmitted by the people who pay me.)"

- "In lesson five I teach that your self-respect should depend on an observer's measure of your worth. My kids are constantly evaluated and judged."

- "In lesson six I teach children that they are being watched. I keep each student under constant surveillance and so do my colleagues. There are no private spaces for children; there is no private time."

These are lessons that an unschooled child never learns, and not one of them will help a child live in joy or contribute to her growing up to be a happy and autonomous adult.

© 2005 Rue Kream

"If you have a garden and a library, you have everything you need."

Marcus Tullius Cicero (106-43 BCE)

Learning to Trust

by Jan Hunt

t's only natural for parents to feel uneasy and uncertain when contemplating a path for their children other than the one they themselves traveled. Those of us who decide to unschool — even when we are convinced that this is the best option for our child — must unlearn many unfounded assumptions about learning that we were conditioned to believe for so many years. If we can do that, we can rediscover the natural love of learning we were born with.

Most of us were taught at school to see a false dichotomy between "learning" and "fun". We came to believe that if it's "educational", it can't be fun, and if it's fun, it can't be learning! A child who is un-schooled from the beginning, as my son Jason has been, enjoys life free of such preconceptions, and continues to see all learning as a wondrous and rewarding experience.

Schools operate under the very different assumption that learning can be imposed from outside the child through various types of coercion, manipulation, rewards and punishments, and that there are distinct deadlines a child "has to" reach or he will never "catch up" (one might ask: catch up with whom, and why?) These are false assumptions, but it can be difficult to let them go when they were so ingrained in our own childhood.

While an understanding of the true spirit of learning comes naturally to Jason, I have had to unlearn many of these assumptions. In that sense, Jason has been my mentor, continually reminding me that learning is not restricted to a specific curriculum, location, time of day, or even to the presence of a "teacher". Jason has taught himself much of what he now uses in his work as our Natural Child Project webmaster and editor.

In a way, we are a generation with a most difficult task, because we are truly forging new trails and gaining new understandings. As I often remind parents in my workshops, unschooling should be much easier when children who were themselves unschooled choose this path for their own children. For these new parents, unschooling will be the norm, and they will have no need to unlearn so many well-meant but harmful beliefs. They will have a much simpler and truer understanding: every child grows at their own natural pace, and, like flower gardeners, parents simply need to trust their children's unique schedules.

Most of us were taught at school
to see a false dichotomy
between "learning" and "fun".

Just as we trust a rose to bloom on its own built-in timetable, so too should we expect children to bloom at their own best pace, and in their own way. There is so much time for a child to grow! If he or she reads fluently at three, at six, or even at twelve, what difference does that really make in the long run? The only real difference it can make is a positive one: a child who is trusted to read when he is ready has the best chance of enjoying a lifetime of pleasurable reading. Yet, because we attended years of school, such understandings can be hard to grasp. Every unschooling parent has likely felt intimidated and unsure at some point. Unschooling is a leap of faith for any parent who attended school in their own childhood.

Jason is now a young adult. When I look back over the years, I see joyful, enthusiastic learning that I have been privileged to share. It has been a happy experience that couldn't have been further from the six hours of drudgery that I had first imagined it would be! Jason not only enjoys learning many things, he sees learning as an interesting, integral part of all life, not a separate activity confined to specific locations, days, or times. In that sense, he is still unschooling and always will be. For Jason, this path has been far more than just an alternative to formal schooling; it has prepared him to live a life full of curiosity and wonder.

Living is learning.

As John Holt once wrote, "Living is learning." This statement appears in an engaging collection of Holt's letters called *A Life Worth Living*. Judging from my own experience, I believe that unschooling is a leap worth taking, one that can lead to a life worth living. But this leap does not need to be attempted alone. Unschooling friends and support groups, books, articles, and websites can be very enlightening. But most of all, we can allow our child to teach us how joyful and natural learning can be. For instruction on unschooling, our children are the single best source of encouragement, inspiration, and reassurance we can have.

"Coercion or compulsion never brings about growth. It is freedom that accelerates evolution."

Paramahansa Yogananda

Every Waking Hour

by John Holt

A mong the many things I have learned about children, learned by many, many years of hanging out with them, watching carefully what they do, and thinking about it, is that children are natural learners.

The one thing we can be sure of, or surest of, is that children have a passionate desire to understand as much of the world as they can, even what they cannot see and touch, and as far as possible to acquire some kind of skill, competence, and control in it and over it. Now this desire, this need to understand the world and be able to do things in it, the things the big people do, is so strong that we could properly call it biological. It is every bit as strong as the need for food, for warmth, for shelter, for comfort, for sleep, for love. In fact, I think a strong case could be made that it might be stronger than any of these.

A hungry child, even a tiny baby who experiences hunger as real pain, will stop eating or nursing or drinking if something interesting happens, because that little child wants to see what it is. This curiosity, this desire to make some kind of sense out of things, goes right to the heart of the kind of creatures that we are.

Children are natural learners.

Children are not only extremely good at learning, they are much better at it than we are. As a teacher, it took me a long time to find this out. I was an ingenious and resourceful teacher, clever about thinking up lesson plans and demonstrations and motivating devices and all of that ackamarackus. And I only very slowly and painfully — believe me, painfully — learned that when I started teaching less, the children started learning more.

I can sum up in five to seven words what I eventually learned as a teacher. The seven-word version is: Learning is not the product of teaching. The five-word version is: Teaching does not make learning. As I mentioned before, organized education operates on the assumption that children learn only when and only what and only because we teach them. This is not true. It is very close to one hundred percent false.

Teaching does not make learning.

Learners make learning. Learners create learning. The reason that this has been forgotten is that the activity of learning has been made into a product called "education", just as the activity, the discipline, of caring for one's health has become the product of "medical care", and the activity of inquiring into the world has become the product of "science", a specialized thing presumably done only by people with billions of dollars of complicated apparatus. But health is not a product and science is something you and I do every day of our lives. In fact, the word *science* is synonymous with the word *learning*.

What do we do when we make learning, when we create learning? Well, we observe, we look, we listen. We touch, taste, smell, manipulate, and sometimes measure or calculate. And then we wonder. We say, "Well, why this?" or "Why is it this way?" or "Did this thing make this thing happen?" or "What made this thing happen?" or "Can we make it happen differently or better?" or "Can we get the Mexican bean beetle off the beans?" or "Can we raise more fruit?" or "Can we fix the washing machine?" or whatever it might be. And then we invent theories, what scientists call hypotheses; we make hunches. We say, "Well, maybe it's because of this", or "Perhaps it's because of that", or "Maybe if I do this, this will happen." And then we test these theories or these hypotheses.

We may test them simply by asking questions of people we think know more than we do, or we may test them by further observation. We may say, "Well, I don't quite know what that thing is, but maybe if I watch it longer I will find out." Or maybe we do some kind of planned experiment — "Well, I'll try putting this on the beans and see if it does something to the bean beetles", or "I'll try doing something else." And from these, in various ways, we either find out that our hunch was not so good, or perhaps that it was fairly good, and then we go on, we observe some more, we speculate some more. We ask more questions, we make more theories, we test them.

This process creates learning, and we all do it. It's not just done by people at MIT or Rensselaer Polytechnic. We do it. And this is exactly what children do. They are hard at work at this process all their waking hours. When they're not actually eating and sleeping, they're creating knowledge. They are observing, thinking, speculating, theorizing, testing, and experimenting — all the time — and they're much better at it than we are. The idea, the very idea, that we can teach small children how to learn has come to me to seem utterly absurd.

---

*Children learn from anything
and everything they see.*

As I was writing this, there came, as if by wonderful coincidence, a long letter from a parent. At one point she says something that is so good that it could be a title for this book: "Every Time I think of Something to Teach Them They Already Know It."

Children learn from anything and everything they see. They learn wherever they are, not just in special learning places. They learn much more from things, natural or made, that are real and significant in the world in their own right and not just made in order to help children learn; in other words, they are more interested in the objects and tools we use in our regular lives than in almost any special learning materials made for them. We can best help children learn, not by deciding what we think they should learn and thinking of ingenious ways to teach it to them, but by making the world, as far as we can, accessible to them, paying serious attention to what they do, answering their questions — if they have any — and helping them explore the things they are most interested in, The ways we can do this are simple and easily understood by other people who like children and will take the trouble to pay some attention to what they do and think about what it may mean. In short, what we need to know to help children learn is not obscure, technical, or complicated, and the materials we can use to help them lie ready to hand all around us.

Editors

Jan Hunt is the Director of The Natural Child Project at naturalchild.org, a member of the Board of Directors for the Canadian Society for the Prevention of Cruelty to Children, and a member of the Advisory Boards for Attachment Parenting International and Child-Friendly Initiative.

Jason Hunt, Jan's son, co-edited and designed the layout for this book. He is the designer and webmaster of naturalchild.org and the Global Children's Art Gallery, and has helped edit much of Jan's writing, including her book *The Natural Child*. He has unschooled all of his life.

Publisher

The Natural Child Project, established in 1996, provides information and support for attachment parenting, natural learning, and child advocacy.

Our website offers articles and advice by leading writers on parenting, unschooling, and child advocacy. The site also features parenting quotes, recommended books, related resources, the Attachment Parenting Family Directory, and the Global Children's Art Gallery. Our online shop offers many unique items for parents and children.

Our vision is a world in which all children are treated with dignity, respect, understanding, and compassion. In such a world, every child can grow into adulthood with a generous capacity for love and trust.

naturalchild.org

Contributors

Nanda Van Gestel is a long-time unschooling mom of four sons living in the Netherlands. She believes that raising children, with as much love and freedom as possible, is the most fulfilling and important job in the world. Nanda enjoys writing about unschooling, motherhood, freedom and love.

Jan Hunt is a parenting counselor and the author of *The Natural Child: Parenting From the Heart* and the children's book *A Gift for Baby*. She has published articles in numerous journals and parenting publications, as well as her own website at naturalchild.org.

Daniel Quinn is best known as the author of the highly acclaimed *Ishmael*. Other works offering inspired solutions to global challenges include *The Story of B, My Ishmael, Beyond Civilization, After Dachau, The Holy, Tales of Adam,* and *If They Give You Lined Paper, Write Sideways.* For more information visit ishmael.org.

Rue Kream is living happily ever after with her husband, Jon, and two children, Dagny and Rowan. Rue is a passionate advocate of unschooling and respectful parenting. Her insightful first book, *Parenting A Free Child: An Unschooled Life*, is available at freechild.info.

Earl Stevens was a founder of the Southern Maine Home Education Support Network and an advocate for unschooling in Maine and nationally for many years. He has been a popular columnist in *Home Education Magazine* and a writer for his own publication, *Talk About Learning*.

Kim Houssenloge lives with her husband Mark and son Lewis in a small country town on the far south coast of New South Wales, Australia, where they have followed a natural learning approach from the start.

John Holt was a pioneer of the American unschooling movement, editor of *Growing Without Schooling*, and a leading advocate of unschooling and children's rights. An eloquent writer, John's many celebrated books include *How Children Learn, Teach Your Own*, and *Learning All the Time*.

Mary Van Doren, her husband Mark, and their daughters Helen, Greta, Alice and Veronica are long-time unschoolers living in Ohio. Mary is currently working as a children's librarian. She and Mark are former Board members of *Growing Without Schooling*.

How to Order this Book

Order online: naturalchild.org/shop

Order by phone: 877-593-1547

About this book: naturalchild.org/unmanual

Email us: naturalchild.org/contact

Counseling with Jan

Jan Hunt, M.Sc. Counseling Psychology, has over twenty years of experience as a counselor and writer on attachment parenting and unschooling, and is the author of *The Natural Child: Parenting from the Heart* and *A Gift for Baby*. She offers telephone counseling worldwide, with a focus on solutions that meet the needs of both parents and children.

Jan would be happy to talk with you! For more information or to schedule a session, write to jan@naturalchild.org.

naturalchild.org/counseling

Also available from naturalchild.org

The Natural Child by Jan Hunt
Paperback and Audio

A Gift for Baby by Jan Hunt
Art by Sunny Rosanbalm

Children's Art Prints,
Cards, and Clothing

Parenting for a Peaceful World
by Robin Grille

Custom Hand-Made
Nursing Dolls

Parenting Cards
100 Gentle Reminders

naturalchild.org/shop

"Parents have a prior right to choose the kind of education that shall be given to their children."

United Nations
Universal Declaration of Human Rights